Titles in this series

Australia	India
Brazil	Italy
Canada	Japan
The Caribbean	The Netherlands
China	New Zealand
France	Nigeria
Germany	Pakistan
Great Britain	Spain
Greece	The U.S.A.

Cover *In Venice most transport is by water. This is part of the Grand Canal.*

Opposite *Tourists enjoying the sunshine at one of the cafés in St Mark's Square, Venice.*

First published in 1989 by
Wayland (Publishers) Ltd
61 Western Road, Hove
East Sussex BN3 1JD, England

© Copyright 1989 Wayland (Publishers) Ltd

Editor: Joan Walters
Series design: Malcolm Smythe

British Library Cataloguing in Publication Data
Powell, Jillian
  1. Italy
  I. Title II. Davey, Julia III. Series
  945.092'8

HARDBACK ISBN 1-85210-049-4

PAPERBACK ISBN 0-7502-1316-7

Typeset by Dorchester Typesetting Group Ltd
Printed in Italy by G. Canale C.S.p.A., Turin

COUNTRIES OF THE WORLD

ITALY

LEARNING
SUPPORT
SERVICES

City College
NORWICH

Please return on or before the
last date stamped below

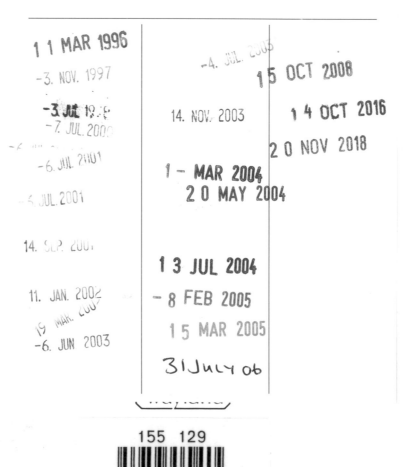

Contents

Words that appear in **bold** in the text are explained in the glossary on page 46.

1 Introducing Italy

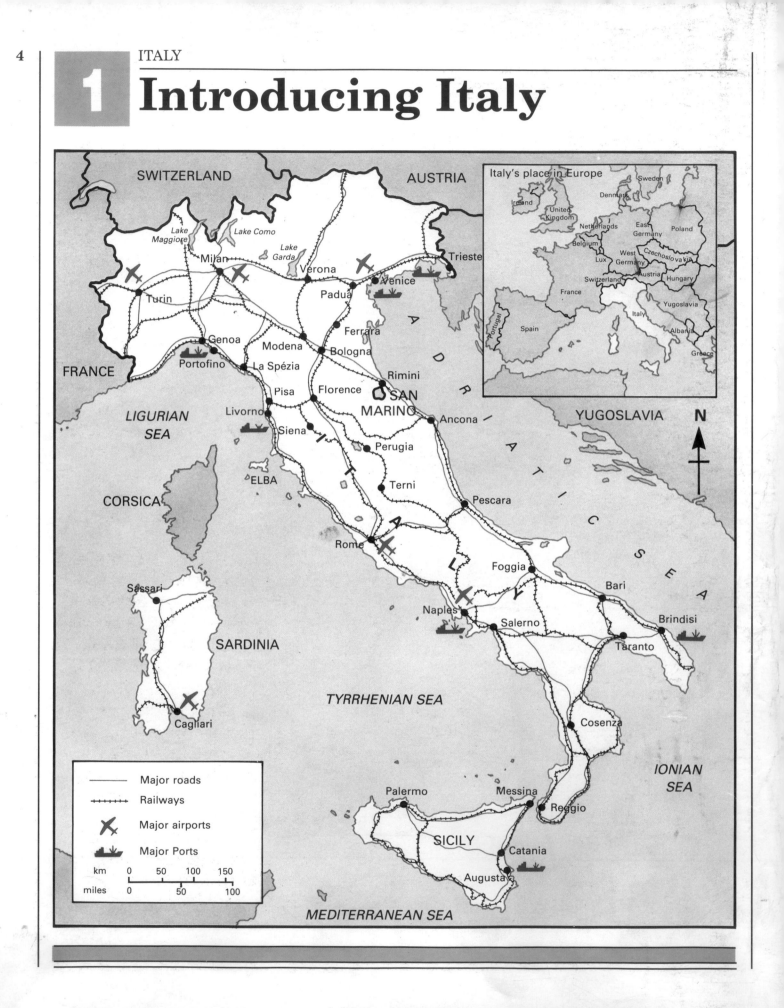

Left The Leaning Tower of Pisa, one of Italy's most famous tourist attractions.

Italy is situated in the Mediterranean region of southern Europe. The long **peninsula** is shaped like a high-heeled boot, which is 'kicking away' the island of Sicily. Four seas surround Italy: the Ligurian and Tyrrhenian seas to the west, the Adriatic to the east, and the Ionian to the south. To the north, the Alps divide Italy from her nearest European neighbours, France, Switzerland, Austria and Yugoslavia; to the south is the African continent.

Italy stretches 1,200 km from north to south and covers an area of 301,278 sq km. The country is divided into twenty regions and ninety-five provinces and includes two tiny independent states: the Vatican City in Rome, and the **Republic** of San Marino, a hill-town on the Adriatic coast. Italian territory includes the two large islands of Sicily and Sardinia, and a number of smaller islands such as Capri and Elba.

Italy's beautiful and varied countryside has inspired generations of artists, and it was here that the **Renaissance** began in the fifteenth century. Renaissance writers and artists were influenced by the great **classical** civilizations of Greece and Rome. Everywhere in Italy there is evidence of the rich classical past, from mighty Roman arches and **amphitheatres**, to delicate wall paintings and **mosaics**.

Although Italy is famous for its art, **archaeology** and history, it is also a leading industrial and agricultural country today. In 1957, Italy became a founder-member of the **European Economic Community** (EEC) and recent years have seen a spectacular growth in its economy, making it one of the richest industrialized countries in the world. The talent of Italian designers, especially in engineering, cars, clothing and interior design, is admired worldwide.

Italy is also famous for the art of **opera** and for its good food and wine. Among its most famous exports are the popular dishes of pasta and pizza.

2 Land and climate

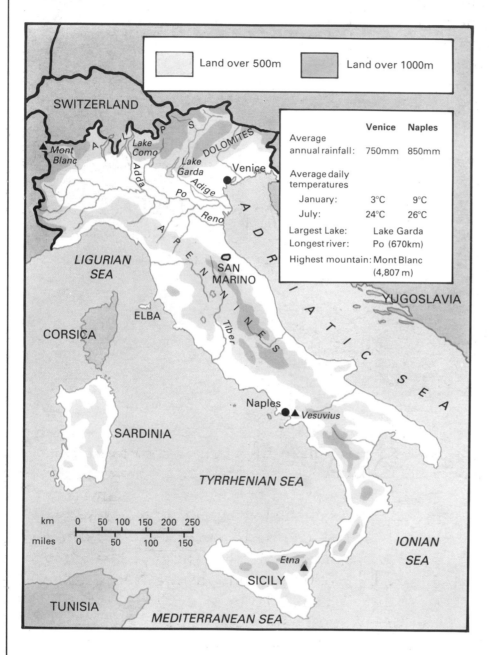

	Venice	Naples
Average annual rainfall:	750mm	850mm
Average daily temperatures		
January:	3°C	9°C
July:	24°C	26°C
Largest Lake:	Lake Garda	
Longest river:	Po (670km)	
Highest mountain:	Mont Blanc (4,807 m)	

Map labels: SWITZERLAND, ALPS, Mont Blanc, Lake Como, Lake Garda, DOLOMITES, Adda, Adige, Po, Reno, Venice, APENNINES, LIGURIAN SEA, SAN MARINO, ELBA, CORSICA, Tiber, ADRIATIC SEA, YUGOSLAVIA, Naples, Vesuvius, SARDINIA, TYRRHENIAN SEA, IONIAN SEA, SICILY, Etna, TUNISIA, MEDITERRANEAN SEA

Legend: Land over 500m — Land over 1000m

km 0 50 100 150 200 250
miles 0 50 100 150

Grapes are grown in many parts of Italy. This vineyard is in Tuscany.

The length of Italy means that there are dramatic contrasts of land and climate. The northern Alpine regions have cold, snowy winters and short summers. The far south and Sicily have hot, dry weather most of the year. Although the northern plains have a continental climate, with cold winters and hot summers, most of Italy enjoys a Mediterranean climate with hot, dry summers, mild winters and rain in the spring and autumn.

Over three-quarters of the country is hilly or mountainous. There are the high, snowy peaks of the Alps and the Dolomites in the north, the Apennines running like a spine down the centre, and the live **volcanoes** of Vesuvius and Etna in the south. Mount Etna (3,340 m), on Sicily, is Europe's largest volcano.

Above The plains and mountains of Sardinia, where the land is parched in summer.

Left The snow-peaked Alps of northern Italy.

On the border with France is the highest mountain in Europe, Mont Blanc (4,807 m). The Alps stretch for 1,300 km along the northern borders. This is a landscape of high, rocky peaks, steep **glaciers** and fast-flowing rivers, fir and pine forests and green valleys. In the foothills are the Italian lakes, including Lake Garda (the largest in Italy), Lake Como and Lake Maggiore.

Left Lake Maggiore, with Isola Bella (the Beautiful Island) in the distance.

The coastline between Amalfi and Atrani in south-west Italy.

South of the Alps are the flat plains between the Po River and Venice. These **fertile**, **alluvial** plains are laced by rivers and streams. The Po is Italy's largest river, and begins in the western Alps, emptying into the Adriatic Sea. Here, in the Po and Adige **deltas**, the land is low-lying and sometimes floods. Lagoons (*lido*) are separated from the sea by sandspits. Venice is built on a series of islands and mud flats in one of these lagoons.

In contrast, the north-west coast is rocky and uneven, jutting out steeply and curving into sheltered sandy bays. It is here, along the Riviera of the Ligurian coast, that some of Italy's most picturesque fishing villages and coastal resorts are to be found, such as Portofino and Portovenere.

Stretching from the Ligurian coast and the Alps in the north, is the rugged Apennine mountain range, the 'backbone' of Italy. In the wildest parts, like the Abruzzi, the climate and the landscape are harsh, with narrow gorges, sharp chalky ridges and windswept plateaux.

The Apennines zigzag southwards to the Strait of Messina, between Sicily and the 'toe' of Italy. Here, in the southernmost regions of Apulia, Basilicata and Calabria, is a varied landscape of dry plains, mountains and high cliffs plunging to sandy beaches and underwater **grottoes**.

To the west are the Mediterranean islands of Sicily and Sardinia. Here too the landscape is rugged and the coastline uneven, with deep inlets and caves. Mountain slopes are covered with the fragrant Mediterranean plants, which in spring give off the scent of eucalyptus, myrtle and roses.

The beauty of these islands contrasts with the gentler landscape of Tuscany and Umbria. Here, the rolling hills and plains are covered with vines and olive trees, fringed with umbrella pines and cypresses.

View over the rooftops of San Gimignano, Tuscany. This fortressed hill-town is famous for its many towers, built by feuding families during the Middle Ages.

3 Wildlife

Wild boar still roam free on Sardinia.

Urban development and hunting have greatly reduced native wildlife in Italy. Large wild game has almost disappeared, although wild boar still live on the Mediterranean **macchia** of Sardinia, and the brown bear, now a protected species, survives in the Trentino and Abruzzi regions.

Other species are protected in Italy's five major national parks and nature reserves, such as the *Gran Paradiso* in Aosta, where the mountain ibex (a kind of wild goat) roams freely. Other large mammals, including the chamois (a goat antelope) and the roe deer, are found in Alpine regions. Here there are also a number of animals like marmots which **hibernate**, and others that change their protective colouring according to the season, like the ermine and the Alpine rabbit. Foxes are also found in the Alps and other high mountain regions, while wolves have retreated to the remotest parts of the central southern Apennines.

Italy also provides **habitats** for a variety of **reptiles** and numerous small **rodents** such as the hare and the squirrel. At Mount Circeo, on the coast of Latium, a national park has been established to protect the mountain, the marshy lagoons and the large colonies of waterbirds and other wildlife that live here. Among birds of prey, the hawk is still common, but the eagle is increasingly rare. There is a wide variety of freshwater and salt-water fish in Italy's rivers and seas, but all are threatened by **pollution** as in other industrialized countries.

A mountain goat in the Gran Paradiso *nature reserve.*

Grey wolves in the Abruzzo.

4 The colourful past

The rich art and culture of Italy reflect its ancient past. Before the Roman Empire, which was established in 27 BC, there were many different tribes and peoples living in Italy.

The Greeks arrived in Italy in the eighth century BC, settling on the southern coasts and on Sicily. They founded wealthy colonies and cities such as Naples, Paestum and Brindisi. This area came to be known as *Magna Graecia* or Great Greece.

At about the same time, the Etruscans settled in Tuscany. They are believed to have come from the East, and archaeological evidence shows that they were an advanced civilization, with organized political, social and religious systems. They were also skilled artists and craftspeople.

Important Dates

753 BC	Foundation of Rome by Romulus.
31	Augustus becomes first Roman Emperor.
AD 395	Empire divided into East (Constantinople) and West (Rome).
476	Collapse of Western Roman Empire.
800	Charlemagne becomes first Holy Roman Emperor.
1309-77	French pressure establishes Clement V as Pope and moves the Papacy to Avignon, France.
1527	Sack of Rome by the troops of the Constable of Bourbon.
1796	Napoleon Bonaparte's first Italian Campaign in Lombardy.
1831	Foundation of the Young Italy movement by Mazzini: growth of national feeling against Austria: the *Risorgimento*.
1870	Rome becomes the capital of Italy. Italian unity is complete.
1915	Italy enters the First World War on the side of the Allies.
1922	Mussolini takes control of the Italian Government.
1925	Mussolini becomes dictator of Italy.
1929	Independence of the Holy See established.
1940	Italy enters the Second World War against Britain and France.
1943	Fall and arrest of Mussolini. Italy changes sides and fights with the Allies against Germany.
1946	Proclamation of the Republic after the Italian people vote against the Monarchy.
1957	Italy becomes a founder-member of the European Economic Community (EEC).
1978	Assassination of Prime Minister Aldo Mori by a terrorist group.
1980	Bologna Railway Station bombed by terrorists.
1985	Agreement signed giving all religions the same status and legal equality.

Left The Colosseum at Rome, the great arena where Romans watched colourful games and spectacles.

Below The triumphal arch of Constantine, in Rome, was built by the Romans.

The Romans settled in the Latium region in central Italy from the middle of the eighth century. Rome's power spread from a city to a vast empire, extending across Europe and the Middle East and lasting for hundreds of years. Hadrian's Wall, in northern England, marks the farthest boundaries of Rome's power in Britain. The Romans were outstanding architects and engineers and there are important Roman remains to be seen throughout Italy.

In the fifth century, German invaders conquered Rome and the Western Roman Empire collapsed. Italy suffered repeated invasions by foreign tribes and the country became divided. Centuries of conflict and upheaval followed and there were frequent clashes between the Pope in Rome and the Holy Roman Emperor in Constantinople (now Istanbul in Turkey).

In spite of these troubles, a number of cities began to grow richer and more powerful through trade. But there were frequent bloody power struggles within and between the rival city-states. This unrest led to further invasions by neighbouring countries, first France and Spain, and then Austria. Italy remained divided into separate kingdoms and city-states until the nineteenth century.

5 The Italian people

Sicilian fishermen sort their nets.

Italy has a population of over 57 million people, making her one of the most heavily populated countries in Europe, after the German Federal Republic and Britain. However, many mountainous and other rural areas remain under-populated, with the highest population concentrated in major cities like Rome, Milan and Turin, and across the Po-Venetian plains and other low-lying areas.

Since the Second World War (1939-45) the number of people living in country areas has steadily dropped, with people moving to the cities to find work. After the war, many people moved from the poorer south and north-east to the north-west, where industry was expanding. This led to a mixing of peoples from the north and south, but even today there tend to be differences between northerners, who are generally taller and fairer in colouring, and southerners, who are generally shorter and darker.

Over the last hundred years many Italians have moved abroad and today there are large Italian communities in such countries as the USA, Australia and Canada. Wherever they live the majority of Italian people are united by the Italian language and by the Roman Catholic religion. However, within Italy there are many regional differences in **dialect**, lifestyle and customs. There are also small groups of people who speak German, French, Greek and Albanian in border regions. Each region has its own traditional costume, crafts and folk festivals. Two famous events are the Venetian Carnival held in February, and the *Palio*, a horse race in Siena in which the winning team is presented with an ancient flag or *palio*. There is even a 'Festival of Noses' held in Soragna, where people compete for the title 'King of Noses'!

The spirit and sense of fun with which people celebrate these festivals is typical of Italians, who are by nature warm and outgoing, showing their emotions freely, through expressive faces and hand gestures.

Right *After school, a group of children meet in town before going to a pizzeria.*

Pageant and history: the annual Regatta along the Grand Canal, Venice.

ITALY

6 Rome

Rome, once capital of the Roman Empire and now capital of Italy, is the centre of political, cultural and religious life. According to legend, Rome was founded in 753 BC by Romulus, who with his twin brother Remus was nursed by a she-wolf. Ancient Rome was built on seven hills situated on the left bank of the River Tiber, but modern Rome has since spread outwards, becoming Italy's largest city.

Nearly three million people live in Rome today and millions more visit the city every year to view the magnificent classical remains and treasure houses. At the centre of Rome is the Forum, the ancient political and civic centre of Imperial Rome, with its ruined streets, arches, temples and palaces. Nearby is the Colosseum, dating from the first century AD. This vast stadium once held up to 50,000 spectators watching the games and **gladiators**. Other famous classical remains include the Pantheon, the round church built as a temple to the classical gods, Trajan's Column (AD 113) and the Appian Way.

Today these important remains exist alongside the shops and offices of modern Rome and, as in other Italian cities, the government has had to protect them from damage caused by the vibration and pollution of heavy traffic.

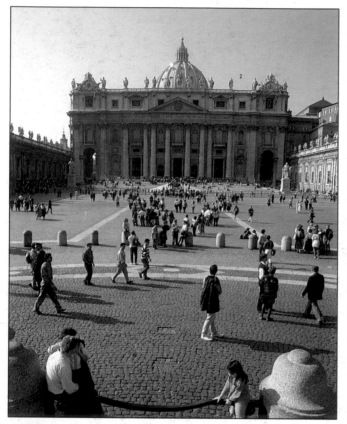

Above The famous St Peter's Basilica (church) is visited by many tourists and pilgrims.

Below Many people stop to rest on Rome's famous Spanish Steps.

A statue of the she-wolf nursing Romulus and Remus. It is said that Romulus founded Rome in 753 BC.

Rome is also a thriving modern city, sometimes noisy and congested, always lively.

Away from tourist attractions, like St Peter's Square in the Vatican, are narrow alleyways leading to cool paved squares where church bells ring and cats lie in the shade. Tourists, too, can seek shade from the hot summer sun by resting at one of the many cafés which are set out under plane trees along elegant streets like the Via Vittorio Veneto,

Above A shady pavement café in Rome where tourists can take a break from sightseeing and enjoy a typical Italian meal of pasta or pizza.

with its grand hotels, airline offices and government buildings. At the height of the season, tourists of every nationality swell Rome's population, crowding over the Spanish steps in the Piazza di Spagna, or pausing to toss a coin into the Trevi fountain, following the belief that if they do, they are sure to return to Rome.

7 Growing up in the city

A modern 4-storey apartment block.

Italians have lived in apartment blocks for centuries. In fact, it was Roman engineers who designed the first 'high-rise' blocks. The average family rents or owns a two- or three-bedroom apartment, sometimes with garage space. Most apartments have balconies, where plants can be grown and the washing can be hung out to dry.

Children may share a bedroom, and use the same room for doing their homework or playing with friends. The living room is where the family relax, watch television or play cards.

At meal times, the whole family will sit down together. Breakfast (*prima colazione*) is usually a simple meal, with bread and jam or pastries (*paste*), and a hot drink like tea, coffee or chocolate. Lunch (*colazione*) is the main meal of the day. Shops and offices close for a siesta, or rest period, of two hours or more. Many children finish school at one o'clock, and come home for lunch which may be a pasta dish, followed by meat or fish served with vegetables or salad, and finally fresh fruit or pastries. Wine and mineral water may be drunk at lunch and with the evening meal. Sometimes, especially for children, the wine is mixed with water. The evening meal (*pranzo*) is usually a lighter meal. It might start with soup, such as *minestre in brodo*, in which pasta or rice is cooked in a savoury stock, then ham or cheese with salad or vegetables, and fresh fruit to follow.

Above The family gets together for lunch in a town apartment. Lunch is usually the main meal of the day.

Right After school and at weekends children meet their friends to go cycling in the park – one of their favourite activities.

Once children have finished their afternoon homework, they may read, listen to music or watch television. Another favourite way of spending family time together is to go for an evening stroll (*la passeggiata*) through the town. Young people might go to the cinema, or meet at a pizzeria (pizza restaurant) for a drink and a chat.

Weekends are an important time for family get-togethers, perhaps with grandparents. Many families choose to escape the city and go out into the country for a walk or a bicycle ride.

8 Life in the country

Above Grandparents, parents and children, not forgetting the dog, often live together in the country.

Less than half the population of Italy now lives in the country, but there are still small rural communities where old traditions, such as making the haystacks or burning wood for charcoal, survive. Families living in the country tend to live in houses rather than apartments, and often grandparents will live in the same household, or close by. If the family runs a farm or smallholding, everyone from children to grandparents will share in the daily tasks. These depend on the type of farm, whether for example vines and olives or wheat are grown, or livestock is reared.

Children living on a farm might have to get up at 6.30 in the morning to feed the chickens or the pigs before going to school. There may be cows or goats to milk, or crops to harvest.

Grapes are harvested in October, and olives a month or so later. At these busy times, all the family will work together, perhaps with help from the village, for a successful harvest. The family may also make some wine to drink at home, or press oil from the olives. On a smallholding, the pig is killed in December, to provide meat for hams and salamis (sausages).

Above Maria-Rosaria and Daniella feeding the chickens on their smallholding.

Above One of 10-year-old Antonio's morning tasks is to feed the pigs.

Younger children living in the country usually attend a local village school. Older children may have to take the public bus, or a school bus from remote areas, to reach the *Scuola Media* (Middle School) in a town nearby. They are likely to spend more of their time outdoors than town children, and although there may not always be cinemas, pizzerias and cafés to visit nearby, a child in the country will have much more space to explore and to play in. The air is cleaner than in the towns, and the countryside may be beautiful. Nevertheless, many young people now move to the towns to look for work, as the Italian economy has shifted from agriculture to industry.

9 Education

Most children in Italy attend state-run schools, although there are also private schools, most of which are run by the Roman Catholic Church. Italian children receive eight years of free and **compulsory** education, starting at the age of six. Parents can choose whether or not to send their three- to five-year-olds to nursery school. Some of these younger children wear a school uniform, which is usually a simple smock or overall.

School starts early at 8.00 am and finishes at 1.00 pm. There is school on Saturday mornings too, but for most children the afternoons are free, although there is usually homework to be completed in time for the next day. Some schools are now offering afternoon schooling as well, and full-time pupils will stay on for school lunch before taking further lessons or afternoon sports.

At the age of eleven, pupils take written and spoken tests before going on to a *Scuola Media*. Here they can take a wide range of subjects including Italian, geography, history, maths, science and technical education and English or French.

Below A technical education class at a Scuola Media.

Above At lunchtime, school is over for many pupils at this Scuola Media.

Right Three friends working together on a class project.

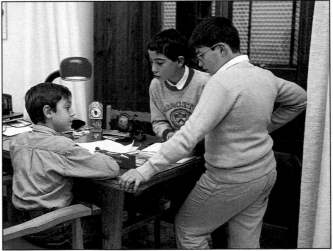

There is usually one hour of religious education each week, although children do not have to attend. Pupils also have two or three hours of sport every week.

If pupils wish to continue their schooling after the age of fourteen they must take further examinations before entering a *Liceo*, or Senior High School, where they may study for up to five years. Some will choose to go on to university and perhaps a teacher-training college; others will take a technical, business, industrial or agricultural course.

There are universities in many Italian cities including Rome, Pisa, Naples and Milan. Bologna University was founded in 1135 and is one of the oldest universities in the world. University students study for between four and six years.

10 Shopping

A jewellery shop on the Ponte Vecchio, the famous shop-lined bridge in Florence.

In Italy, as in other western countries, supermarkets and self-service stores have, in recent years, become popular and convenient ways of shopping. As well as larger stores in town or city centres, there are now a number of hypermarkets or giant supermarkets where it is possible to buy almost everything at one place.

Nevertheless, even in the larger cities, the small specialist shop or general store is still popular and common in Italian streets. These shops are often family-run, and offer the customer personal service. There are various specialist food shops, such as the *pasticceria*, selling cakes and pastries, the *panetteria* or bakery, the *frutteria*, or greengrocers, and the *gelateria*, or ice-cream shop. Smaller towns and villages are likely to have a general food store, usually called *alimentari*.

Italians like to cook with fresh ingredients. They shop daily for meat, salad, fish, pasta and bread. As well as specialist shops, many towns hold colourful street markets every day, with the stalls selling a variety of fresh produce, such as fish, meat, local cheeses, salamis (sausages), fruit and vegetables.

In wealthy cities such as Rome, Milan and Turin, there are a number of elegant shopping streets where specialist shops offer expensive quality goods: clothes, linen, leather goods and shoes. These include the Via Condotti in Rome, the Via Montenapoleone in Milan and the Via Roma in Turin.

Most shops close at lunchtime, rolling down blinds and shutters, and stay closed until as late as 4.00 pm. However, they stay open until eight o'clock in the evening, and many people out on 'la passeggiata' will do their shopping in the late afternoon and early evening.

Right An ice-cream stand in Venice. Italy is famous for its delicious ice-cream.

Below Open markets like this are a favourite place for buying fruit and vegetables.

11 Sport and leisure

The most popular sports in Italy include soccer, bicycle racing, boxing, and car and motorbike racing. Every Sunday afternoon, football stadiums all over Italy are packed for the National Championship league games. Among the most successful teams are Juventus and Roma. Children learn soccer at school, and often play in their free time, either in a park, or just in a street or courtyard. At school, boys and girls play team games such as volleyball, basketball and softball, and all pupils take gym or athletics.

In Italy, people can ride a scooter from the age of fourteen.

Left *A game of football in the park.*

Cycling is a very popular sport among all age groups. On Sundays, groups of cyclists take to the roads in their brightly-coloured, skin-tight racing gear. The best will enter the *Giro d'Italia*, the national cycling race held every spring. For others, bicycles are for riding around the park with friends, on free afternoons or weekends. Motorbikes and scooters are also very popular, especially in towns, and a young person can ride a small motorbike or scooter from the age of fourteen.

Grand Prix racing at the Monza Circuit near Milan.

Car racing is a popular spectator sport. The Italian Grand Prix is held every year at the world-famous Monza circuit near Milan. Events like this can also be watched on television. In Italy there are three state channels, *Raiuno*, *Raidue* and *Raitre*, and many more commercial stations. The average town will receive about forty different channels, offering news, films, documentaries, sports and cartoons.

Watching television or playing cards are popular family activities in the evenings and at weekends. In the afternoons and early evenings, many people like to go for a stroll in the park or in town. Street cafés are popular places for meeting friends, and chatting or reading.

At holiday times, more people stay in Italy than travel abroad. In summer, they can enjoy the warm climate and fine sandy beaches along the Italian Riviera; in winter they can visit resorts in the Alps, Dolomites or Apennines, for winter sports such as skiing.

Left *Skiers enjoying the Alpine slopes.*

12 Religion

The church of St Francis at Assisi, famous for its beautiful frescoes by Giotto, is a place of pilgrimage for many Catholics.

Until recently, Roman Catholicism was the official religion of Italy, but in 1985 a new agreement was signed, giving all religions the same status and legal equality. The Protestant, Jewish and Islamic faiths are all represented in Italy, but eight out of ten people are Roman Catholic.

The Catholic faith still plays an important part in people's lives.

Many families still dress up in their 'Sunday best' to go to church and attend Mass. Italian children usually take their first **communion** and receive **confirmation** when they are eight years old.

Public holidays are held on religious festivals and saints' days throughout the year, and they may be marked by colourful processions and celebrations. They include the Feast of Epiphany (6 January), Ascension Day, St Peter and St Paul (29 June) and All Saints Day (1 November).

There are many beautiful churches in Italy. St Peter's Basilica, in the Vatican City, Rome, is the largest church in the world, visited by thousands of **pilgrims** and tourists every year. The Vatican City is the world centre of the Roman Catholic Church, and has been a free **sovereign state** since 1929, although the **Holy See** recognizes Rome as capital of Italy. The Pope, currently Pope John Paul II, is Head of State.

The Vatican is little larger than New York's Central Park in the USA, and is the smallest 'country' in the world to which other countries send ambassadors. It has its own flag, prints its own newspapers and mints its own coins.

Top The Pope appears at his window in the Vatican at noon on Sundays to speak to the people.

Inset A Swiss guard posted outside St Peter's Basilica, Rome.

Every night the gates to the Vatican are locked by the Swiss Guard, who have guarded the Pope and his palace since 1506. Their colourful uniforms are said to have been designed, like the great dome of St Peter's, by the Renaissance artist Michelangelo.

13 Artistic Italy

Every year, millions of tourists and scholars come to Italy to see the artistic treasures in its churches and museums and in the Italian countryside. There are important Etruscan and Roman remains, **Byzantine** mosaics, **medieval** churches, sculptures and **frescoes**, and outstanding masterpieces in art and architecture of the Renaissance and **Baroque** periods.

Florence, Rome and Venice all have many examples of Renaissance

Florence is the home of many of Italy's most famous works of art. Today, artists still flock to this beautiful city to paint and draw its fine buildings.

Below The Birth of Venus *by Sandro Botticelli can be seen at the Uffizi Gallery in Florence.*

architecture, sculpture and painting, with works by famous artists such as Leonardo da Vinci (1452-1519), Raphael (1483-1520), Titian (c1487-1576), Botticelli (1440-1510) and Michelangelo (1475-1564).

Italy is also the country where the art of **opera** was born. Rossini (1792-1868), Verdi (1813-1901) and Puccini (1858-1924) are all famous Italian composers of opera. *La Scala*, the most famous opera house in the world, is in Milan.

One special form of theatre which developed in Italy in the sixteenth

The Flood, *detail from the Sistine Chapel ceiling frescoes painted by Michelangelo.*

century is the *Commedia dell'Arte*, a comic drama which uses set themes and characters like Harlequin and Columbine.

In the twentieth century, Italy has developed a successful film industry famed for the work of directors like Rossellini, Zeffirelli, Visconti and Fellini as well as for the popular 'spaghetti western'. Rome's Cinecittà studios are the centre of the Italian film industry.

14 Fashion and design

Ferrari is among Italy's most famous makes of car.

For centuries, Italian designers have been famous for their talent and engineering skills. Today Italy is a world-leader in the fields of fashion, engineering and modern industrial design. Italian style is outstanding in the design of streamlined cars, modern furniture, domestic appliances such as fridges and washing machines, and in clothes sold in designer and high street fashion shops.

Below These expensive shops along the Montenapoleone in Milan attract fashion-conscious shoppers.

A programme of 'National Fashion' was launched 150 years ago to bring back ancient traditions of Italian design and textile manufacture, and to compete against foreign imports. The **couture** side of Italian fashion was developed by designers like Rosa Genoni, a seamstress working in Milan in the early twentieth century. She took her design ideas from Italian art. But it was not until the 1950s that Italian *couture* became famous world-wide, when the Florentine Marquis Giovanni Giorgini held a fashion show at his house, showing the work of young designers to the world's press.

Above Gucci leatherware is famous throughout the world.

Above The designer Giorgio Armani, with one of his creations.

Today, Milan is Italy's 'fashion capital', with the Milan *Collezione* (collections) held twice yearly, showing the work of famous designers like Valentino and Giorgio Armani. Fashion is a leading export, with many Italian brand names famous the world over, from Gucci, makers of top quality leather shoes, handbags and belts, to Benetton, popular among the young for their brightly-coloured knitwear and casual clothes.

ITALY

15 Farming, fishing, food

Wheat		Fruit	
Cattle		Vines	
Sheep		Olives	
Rice		Fishing ports	

Although industry has taken the lead from agriculture, growing food still plays an important part in the Italian economy. The differences in land and climate over the length of the country mean that crops and livestock vary from region to region.

Farms in mountainous areas like the Alpine regions of the north tend to be larger. In the summer, sheep or cattle graze on the high pastures, while the lower slopes support vineyards, and smaller farms grow rye, potatoes and fruit. On the flat, fertile Po plains, rice and other cereal crops are grown, and there is good pasture for cattle. In the hot, dry south and on Sicily, where the climate is sub-tropical and there is rich volcanic soil, a variety of vegetables and citrus fruits such as oranges and lemons are grown. Farmers may also grow tobacco and keep goats or sheep.

Selling fish fresh in from the boats on the quayside at Viareggio on the west coast.

Left *Olives ripening in the hot summer sun.*

Despite these regional differences, agriculture in Italy is dominated by wheat, vines and olives. Italy is one of the chief wheat-producing countries in the European Economic Community (EEC), producing flour for bread and for the national dish of pasta. There are said to be some 600 different types of pasta. Spaghetti, lasagne and macaroni are some of the best known, all served with different sauces. Italy is also the world's second largest producer of olive oil, which comes mainly from the olive groves of the south, in Apulia, Calabria and Sicily.

Fish, too, plays an important part in the Italian diet. More than 320 million kg of fish are caught each year and fish dishes are eaten in many parts of the country, especially at seaports such as Venice.

Above *A wine cellar with the casks and* fiaschi *in which the wine matures.*

Left *A butcher's shop, selling salamis,* porchetta *and ham.*

Italy is well known for the quality of its regional cooking and specialities as well as for popular dishes such as pasta, pizza and risotto (a rice-based dish). Among the delicious regional produce are salamis (sausages) from Bologna, prosciutto or Parma ham, and Parmesan cheese, a hard cheese with a strong flavour from the north. Regional specialities include *porchetta*, spit-roasted pork from Umbria and Sardinia, and cassata Siciliana, an ice-cream dessert with chocolate, candied fruit and nuts, from Sicily.

Italy is one of the world's leading wine producers, bottling more sorts of wine than any other nation. Vines are grown in all districts, and wine is drunk daily with meals, sometimes mixed with water. Over 1,000 varieties of wine-producing grapes are used, resulting in many regional differences. It is claimed that there are some 5,000 types of Italian wine.

The best wines come from the northern regions, especially Tuscany, Lombardy, Piedmont and the Veneto. Among the best-known varieties are Chianti from Tuscany, which is sometimes sold in bottles bound in straw, Frascati, a white wine from Latium, and Valpolicella, a light red wine from the Verona district.

Maize (corn) is one of the main cereal crops grown in Italy. It is often harvested by hand.

Italy also produces wine-based drinks such as vermouth, a sweet or dry aperitif (drink to be enjoyed before meals), based on white wine flavoured with herbs, and the dark, **fortified** Marsala from Sicily.

Almost half the farms in Italy specialize in the cultivation of vines. Warm hillsides are ideal for growing vines, and the grapes should ripen in time for a September or October harvest. After the grapes have been harvested and pressed, the juice must be allowed to ferment with yeast and sugar (converting the sugar to alcohol), then put in casks to mature before it is bottled. In Italy, young wine is often drunk the same year, served from *fiaschi* or flasks, but there are also many fine vintage wines (wines which have been allowed to mature).

16 Industry

Since the end of the Second World War in 1945, Italian industrial production has expanded rapidly, making Italy one of the richest and most industrialized countries in the world. Manufacturing industries depend more on a skilled workforce than raw materials because Italy has few natural resources. Energy comes from hydroelectric power stations, natural gas and a small number of nuclear power stations, although some electricity has to be imported.

The main industrial areas are in the north-west 'triangle' (Milan-Turin-Livorno) and across the broad valley of the River Po. Turin is the heart of the Italian motor industry. Here, the leading firm of Fiat makes cars, lorries, tractors and aeroplanes. Lamborghini, Ferrari and Alfa Romeo are other famous Italian makes of car.

Below The Fiat factory at Cassino, to the south-east of Rome. Fiat cars are exported world-wide.

Inset Fiat also make agricultural machinery.

Italy is a leading Common Market producer of electrical household appliances from fridge-freezers to sewing machines, with brand names like Zanussi and Olivetti known world-wide. The steel and metal-working industries are also strong, as are textiles, the oldest Italian industry, which today produces synthetic (man-made) fibres as well as silk, cotton and wool. There are also successful chemical and **pharmaceutical** industries.

In an effort to increase modern development and employment in the south, a finance organization called the *Cassa del Mezzogiorno* was set up. It provided money for land improvement and essential services (roads, water, drainage) and to attract new industries to the area. Trade fairs were organized, and laws passed to provide extra funds for industries such as the steelworks at Taranto, now part of the Taranto-Bari-Brindisi industrial triangle.

Main imports:	Oil, petroleum products, tobacco, other fuels, minerals
Main exports:	Heavy transport machinery, cars, furniture, fashion, domestic equipment, food and wine

Top right *Leather goods for sale in a Florence market.*

Right *Decorative ceramic ware on show at one of Italy's tourist shops. Tourism is an important industry in Italy.*

There has also been some development of tourism in the south. This is now one of Italy's leading industries. Tourism also supports and encourages local arts and crafts. Faenza and Assisi are known for their brightly-painted ceramics; Florence and Sardinia for their leather crafts.

17 Transport

Italian engineers are famous for their roads and railways, linking Italy to its European neighbours by tunnels under the Alps, and crossing deep valleys by vast **viaducts**. Motorists must pay a toll for use of the *autostrade* (motorways) which were the first to be built in Europe.

Most Italian families have at least one car. In the cities, small cars or motorscooters are popular, although many people use public transport to get to work. There are bus companies in each province, and Rome and Milan have tram services as well as Metro or underground rail systems.

Recently, there have been efforts to reduce the damage and pollution caused to historic buildings by modern-day traffic. *Zona Bleu* or 'blue zones' have been introduced, restricting access to essential traffic only.

Above Motorway toll barriers. Motorists take a ticket at the point of entry and pay on leaving the autostrada.

Below An electric tram in Milan.

Trains are a cheap and convenient method of travel in Italy and are used mainly for passenger transport. The state-run railway *Ferrovie dello Stato* connects Italy to Northern Europe by the Trans-Europe Express and other international express trains.

Air transport, both for passengers and **freight**, has grown rapidly in recent years. Almost all major cities have an airport (Rome and Milan have two) and the national airline, Alitalia, has regular flights to eighty-six cities in forty-four countries world-wide.

Above *A gondolier steers his course among the vaporetti on the Grand Canal, Venice.*

Left *Alitalia, Italy's national airline, flies to forty-four countries around the world.*

For travel by sea, passenger liners and merchant ships sail from the main ports around Italy's coast, such as Genoa, Trieste, Naples and Venice. But it is in Venice that Italy's most unusual transport system operates. As the city is built on 117 islands, transport between them is by water. Motorboats, or *vaporetti*, carry the main passenger traffic, while working barges carry freight. There are police boats, red fire-service boats, and black and gold funeral barges. But most popular of all, especially with the tourists, are long, graceful boats called gondolas.

18 Government

Until the late nineteenth century Italy was divided into separate kingdoms, **principates** and **duchies**, with parts occupied by France, Spain and Austria. But the French Revolution of 1789, and the new ideals of freedom and equality spread by Napoleon's armies during the Italian Campaigns in 1796, caused unrest and a new sense of national feeling: the *'Risorgimento'*. There were uprisings from the early nineteenth century, and when a republic was declared in France in 1848, there were mass demonstrations on the streets of Rome, Naples and Turin.

It was not until 1870 that the Italian people's struggle to unite their country finally succeeded. It came about through the leadership of three men: the Piedmontese statesman Count Camillo di Cavour, the revolutionary Giuseppe Mazzini, and the soldier Giuseppe Garibaldi, who urged his volunteer army of 'the Thousand' to 'make Italy or die'.

On 1 July 1870, Rome became capital of a united country, although in 1929 the Vatican became an independent sovereign state, ruled by the Pope. However, the people were still not happy and after the First World War (1914-18) in which Italy fought with the **Allies** against Germany, this unhappiness led to the growth of a powerful political

Above Mussolini delivering a speech in 1935.

movement, **Fascism**. In 1922, the Fascist leader Benito Mussolini became head of the government and three years later he announced a **dictatorship**. During the Second World War (1939-45) Mussolini took sides with Nazi Germany, but before the war was over Italy changed sides and fought with the Allies. Mussolini was captured and killed while trying to escape to Switzerland.

Following elections held in June 1946 to decide whether Italy should become a monarchy (a country ruled by a king or queen) or a republic, a new **constitution** was drawn up, declaring Italy a Democratic

Republic. According to the constitution, the President of the Republic is elected by Parliament for a term of seven years. He appoints the Prime Minister, who runs the government with his Council of Ministers. Parliament has two houses: a Chamber of Deputies, which is directly elected, and the Senate, which is elected on a regional basis.

The leading political parties today are the Christian Democrats, the Communist Party and the Socialist Party. Some thirteen parties fight elections, and their opposition to the government leads to political unrest. As a result of this, there have been no fewer than forty-eight Italian governments since the Second World War.

These policemen in Rome are waiting to go on patrol near St Peter's Square, where barriers have been erected to control the crowds waiting to see the Pope.

Below *The structure of the Italian government.*

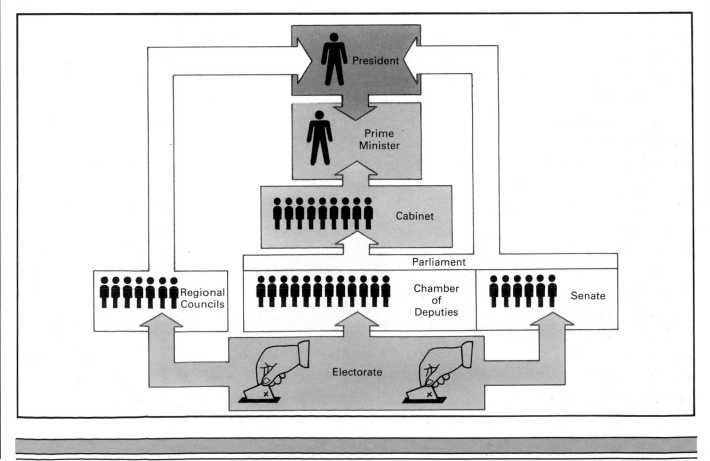

19 Facing the future

This atomic plant south of Rome, and others like it, will provide electricity in the future.

In recent years, the Italian economy has grown very quickly. However, the country spends much more than it earns and this situation is continuing to grow worse. This is because arguments between the different political parties prevent major decisions being made. Often the government is opposed by a **coalition** (joining together of forces) of some of the other political parties. They also face pressure from groups of people trying to enforce political change (terrorists), who are prepared to go to any lengths – bombings, kidnappings and killings – to achieve their aims.

The threat of terrorism is one of the problems Italy shares with other Western nations. Others include the problem of drug abuse among young people in big cities, and a high level of unemployment, especially among the young and in the poorer south. *'La problema del mezzogiorno'*, the problem of the south, has existed for many years and still remains, although much has been done to improve the land and set up new industries. It is here, in Sicily and Calabria, that the powerful organization called the Mafia is based, although Mafia influence has now spread to the north too.

Blackmail, smuggling and street violence are all continuing problems related to the Mafia.

And there are new challenges too. Like other industrialized countries, Italy faces serious problems of pollution affecting its seas and rivers. The need to clean up and protect the environment is one of the major challenges of the late twentieth century.

In spite of these problems, Italy has made remarkable progress in recent years, leading to a rise in living standards for the Italian people.

Above Unemployed people registering at the labour exchange. High unemployment is a problem for many Western nations.

Below A farmer in southern Italy with his goats. In the last 40 years many younger people have moved north to look for work in the cities.

Glossary

Allies Nations fighting on the same side in a war.

Alluvial A fine-grained fertile soil made up of mud, silt and sand that has been deposited by a river.

Amphitheatres Circular, open-air buildings in which rows of seats rise from a central open arena or stage.

Archaeology The study of ancient times and relics.

Baroque The term used to describe the art and architecture of the seventeenth century.

Byzantine The term used to describe the art and architecture of the Eastern Roman Empire.

Classical The style of art and architecture of ancient Greece and Rome.

Coalition A grouping of political parties with some of the same aims or policies.

Communion The most important service of the Roman Catholic and other Churches.

Compulsory Made necessary by rules or laws.

Confirmation A ceremony of the Christian Church, by which people become full members.

Constitution The rules that a government must follow to run a country. The constitution of a country also lays down a citizen's rights.

Couture A French word meaning dressmaking, used to refer to designer fashion and tailoring.

Dialect A form of a language spoken in a particular geographical area.

Delta A triangular piece of land formed by two or more branches of a river at its mouth.

Dictatorship A form of government where one person (a dictator) has absolute rule and does not have to govern according to any laws or opposition.

Duchy Land under the rule of a duke.

Economy The management of money or of financial affairs.

European Economic Community (EEC) A group of twelve European nations working towards economic union. It is also called the Common Market.

Fascism An extreme right-wing political and social movement that is against freedom of the people.

Fertile (of soil) Having enough goodness to support the growth of a large and healthy crop of plants.

Fortified Made strong by the addition of brandy or other alcohol.

Freight The load or cargo carried by ships, aeroplanes, trains and trucks.

Frescoes Paintings on walls or ceilings.

Glaciers Large masses of ice which start from a build-up of snow in a high valley and slowly move down a mountain.

Gladiators Men trained to fight in arenas to provide entertainment in ancient Roman times.

Grottoes Small caves, some of which are half filled with water or have other attractive features.

Habitat The natural environment or home of animals or plants.

Hibernate To sleep during the winter.

Holy See The Papal Court of Rome.

Macchia Mediterranean brushwood vegetation.

Medieval Belonging to the Middle Ages (about AD 500-1400).

Mosaics Designs made up of small pieces of coloured glass or stone.

Opera Musical drama, or plays with some or all of the words set to music.

Peninsula A piece of land almost surrounded by water but connected to the mainland.

Pharmaceuticals Medical drugs and other medicines; from the Greek word 'pharmakon', a drug.

Pilgrims People who make a journey to a sacred place for religious reasons.

Pollution Dangerously high levels of dirt and poisonous substances in air or in water.

Principates Lands ruled by a prince.

Renaissance The revival of arts and learning in Europe during the fifteenth and sixteenth centuries.

Reptiles Any cold blooded, egg-laying animal with horny scales or a shell such as snakes, lizards and turtles.

Republic A nation without a monarch, usually with an elected president as head of state.

Rodents A group of small mammals with constantly growing incisor (front) teeth specially for gnawing their food. The group includes rats, squirrels, mice and marmots.

Sovereign State A state that is independent of outside authority (for example, the Vatican City in Rome is an independent state within Italy).

Viaducts Bridges used to support roads or railways across a valley.

Volcanoes Mountains with an opening in the top from which molten lava, rock fragments, ashes and gases bubble forth.

Books to read

Biucchi, Edwina *Italian Food and Drink* (Wayland, 1986)

Carsaniga, Pamela *Living in Rome* (Wayland, 1984)

Firmian, Giovanni *Matteo Lives in Italy* (Young Library Ltd, 1984)

Leach, Michael *Italy* (Macdonald Educational, 1984)

Mariella, Linzia *Passport to Italy* (Franklin Watts, 1986)

Moon, Bernice and Cliff *Italy is My Country* (Wayland, 1984)

Sproule, Anna *Italy* (Macdonald Educational, 1987)

Zulueta, Tana de *We Live in Italy* (Wayland, 1984)

Picture acknowledgements

All photographs were taken by Julia Davey with the exception of the following: The Bridgeman Art Library 30; Hutchison Library 8; Italian Tourist Board 30; Oxford Scientific Films (R. Villarosa) 11; Topham 10, 16 (bottom), 27 (top), 33 (both), 41 (bottom), 43 (left), 44; A. Walters 27 (bottom); Wayland Picture Library 38, 45; ZEFA 10, 11, 14, 32. Maps and diagrams provided by Peter Bull.

Index